Making the Most of Your Church Wedding

A gift to last a lifetime

Ally Barrett

About this booklet

You're reading this book because you're planning a church wedding. Congratulations! The date and reception venue are fixed, the other details are falling into place, and now it's time to focus on the service itself and preparing for your married life beyond the big day.

You'll have a lot to think about as you plan the service. You'll need to choose readings, hymns and other music, and consider the practicalities, such as banns, rehearsals, fees and more. Your minister will talk you through all the options, and you can also find a wealth of fantastic ideas and useful information on the Church of England weddings website, **http://yourchurchwedding.org**. This site will even play hymns to help you choose!

Meanwhile, the aim of this booklet is to enable you to *make the most* of your wedding day. It uses the words and actions of the marriage service to help you think about life, family, God, relationships, commitment, church and more. Getting to know what you will say and do in church is a great way to prepare for your married life, however long you've been together. You may want to work through the booklet with your minister or by yourselves at home.

A note on icons

The following icons are used in this book:

Excerpts from the wedding service

Things to think about and talk about

Actions – things to do

Speech bubbles with real-life comments.

How does the marriage service work?

The service includes:

- **words** – some of the most beautiful and powerful words that it's possible to say to another person;
- **actions and objects** – these reinforce the words and make them feel more real, acting as a lasting reminder of what you mean to each other and what you are promising;
- the **'stuff of the heart'** – your own thoughts, feelings, hopes, dreams, intentions and memories that you bring to the service;
- the **grace of God** – you are inviting God to your wedding and into your life together, and God is very active in your marriage service and beyond.

By the time you come to your wedding day, this booklet will have helped you connect your emotional and spiritual journey to each word and action of the marriage service, so that you can enjoy God's blessing on you both and on your life together. This means that your wedding is not only a pledge for the future, but also a celebration of everything that you already are.

If, as the day draws closer, you start to feel that everything has to be perfect, remember why you're getting married in the first place. A wedding doesn't have to be perfect to be the best day of your life.

The marriage service and your life

The marriage service is full of significant, life-changing words and actions. It can even seem a bit daunting. But you have chosen to make your marriage vows in God's house and to ask for his blessing on your life together, so during the service there are lots of little prayers. These are reminders that you're not alone: God is with you.

This pattern can also be true of life: we face momentous choices, experience great joys and go through challenging times. And in life, God is with us. Praying can be a great way of celebrating the good things and asking for help with the hard things. So a church wedding is a truly prayerful start to your married life.

What is prayer?
Perhaps praying is something that you are very comfortable with, or perhaps the idea seems strange and new. Prayer is simply contact with God, so prayers might use words, or they might just be thoughts directed towards God. God is better at listening than we are at praying! Think about a time when you have said or thought a prayer:

- when you were worried about something;
- when you had something to say 'Thank you' for;
- when you felt awe about something.

If you're not sure how to start praying, why not ask your minister for some suggestions?

How the service fits together

The Welcome - the entrance of the bride, the opening words and the first hymn

The Preface - what the Church teaches about marriage

The Declarations - the assurance that there is nothing holding you back from entering wholeheartedly into marriage

The Collect - the first of many prayers for your marriage

The Readings - wisdom from the Bible, and a chance to personalize your service with other readings that have special meaning for you

The Sermon/Address - a chance for your minister to give you some encouraging words, usually on themes from the readings you have chosen

The Vows - the famous words of promise

The Giving of Rings - a visible sign of love that never ends (most couples have a ring each, but it is also possible just to use one ring, for the bride)

The Proclamation and Blessing - your marriage sealed by God's blessing

The Registration of the Marriage - a public record of the marriage in the eyes of the law and the community (this might take place at the end of the service instead)

The Prayers - for you, your family, your home and your future

The final Blessing - as you go out into the world as husband and wife, God goes with you and ahead of you.

Entering the church

The first thing that happens in a marriage service is the entrance of the bride. The first words in the service assure us that God loves us and welcomes us just as we are.

The grace of our Lord Jesus Christ,
the love of God,
and the fellowship of the Holy Spirit
be with you
And also with you.
God is love, and those who live in love live in God
and God lives in them.

When we give or receive love, we are experiencing God's greatest gift to the world, whether we realize it or not. Our love for one another shows us a little of what God's love is like.

Most couples find it helpful to come to church as much as they can before the service, so that by the big day they feel really at home. When will you be able to visit your church as a couple, whether for a service or just to spend some time quietly there together?

How do you feel as you come into church?
- Is your church the 'home' church for both of you, or just for one of you? Or is your church new to you both?
- What are your memories and experiences of coming to church, and how does it make you feel?

The Preface: what marriage is about . . .

In the presence of God . . .
we have come together
to witness the marriage of . . . . . . and . . . . . . ,
to pray for God's blessing on them,
to share their joy
and to celebrate their love. . . .
[Marriage] is given
that as man and woman grow together
in love and trust,
they shall be united with one another
in heart, body and mind.

Read through the excerpts from the Preface on this page and the next two pages. Ask yourselves, 'What does marriage mean to us?' Do you agree with how the Church expresses the nature and purpose of marriage?

Separately, write down the top five essential things that marriage means to you: what is marriage for, and why do you feel it's important to get married? Then compare what each of you has written, not to see whose list is 'better', but to learn from each other and enjoy all that each of you brings to the process of preparing for marriage.

. . . for you, for your family, for life . . .

> The gift of marriage brings husband and wife together
> in the delight and tenderness of sexual union
> and joyful commitment to the end of their lives.
> It is given as the foundation of family life
> in which children are [born and] nurtured
> and in which each member of the family,
> in good times and in bad,
> may find strength, companionship and comfort,
> and grow to maturity in love.

Getting married makes your commitment to each other public. People will look at you afresh, so your relationship needs to be a model of how real love looks in real life.

Jointly, write down the top three positive effects that you hope your marriage will have on you or others.

Think about the impact your marriage will have on those around you – your family and friends. Is there anyone who will find your wedding or marriage hard to cope with, or anyone whom you yourselves find difficult? Are you worried about any family conflicts? If you already have children, how will your marriage affect them, and have you talked about it with them? If you don't already have children, have you talked about whether and when you might try to start a family?

. . . and for the world

By getting married you are showing your commitment to each other publicly. You are reminding the world that happiness doesn't come from selfishness, but from self-giving. You are saying that interdependence is a better way of living than independence, and that love can change the world.

Marriage is a sign of unity and loyalty . . . It enriches society and strengthens community.

What might you do in the future, as a married couple, to 'enrich society and strengthen community'? Work out what social issues you both feel strongly about, and look for ways in which you, as a couple, can get more involved in changing the world around you.

Bringing love into the world
Watch the news together and then reflect on these questions:
- Where can you see evidence of love and commitment and generosity, forgiveness and peace?
- Where can you see evidence of hatred and selfishness, conflict, violence and oppression?
- How do you already help make the world a better place?

We help out in a club offering free sports coaching for children on our housing estate.

We volunteer to do the charity collections in our road – so we get to know our neighbours, and it's fun doing it together.

The Declarations: no holding back

The minister asks everyone at the service if they know of any legal reason why you would not be able to marry. This isn't something to worry about - the minister will have explained to you what these reasons might be. He or she then asks you:

The vows you are about to take are to be made in the presence of God, who is judge of all and knows all the secrets of our hearts; therefore if either of you knows a reason why you may not lawfully marry, you must declare it now.

Although the question only asks about *legal* reasons, it's good to remember that in marriage you bring yourself as you really are, with nothing holding you back. Take some time to think about your past, before you became a couple. Is there anything that could stop you entering wholeheartedly into marriage? Are there things you haven't told each other?

- What have you each learnt from any past relationships?
- Do you have 'baggage' that could get in the way of your marriage?

If you think there might be an issue from the past that you need to sort out, don't put it off - start to do it now. If you think you might need help with this, talk to your minister - he or she is there for you.

Love, comfort, honour, protect

Woven through these words is everything you have already shared as a couple, and all that you will share in your future together. The groom answers first:

. . . . will you take . . . . . . to be your wife? Will you love her, comfort her, honour and protect her, and, forsaking all others, be faithful to her as long as you both shall live?
I will.

The bride then makes the same declaration.

What do the words look like in real life?
Talk together about each of the most crucial words. What do they mean to you individually and as a couple? How do they come to life in your relationship? How do you comfort, honour and protect each other?

I WILL

Why not think of practical examples of how these words apply to your relationship. If you're feeling creative, you could draw pictures, or write your thoughts in a love letter.

Love means . . .

Comfort means . . .

Honour means . . .

Protect means . . .

Being faithful means . . .

Support for you in your marriage

Will you, the families and friends of . . . . . . and . . . . . .
support and uphold them in their marriage
now and in the years to come?
We will.

All the people at your wedding have come to support you. You will
have jobs for some of them on the day: ushers, people to do your
readings, witnesses, bridesmaids, best man, and so on. How will you
help everyone to feel included? This is especially important if you
already have children who will want to be part of your special day
(you might want a friend or relative to look after them at the service).

Everyone is there
to help you in your
marriage - so hold them
to their promises!

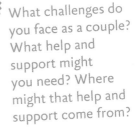

What challenges do
you face as a couple?
What help and
support might
you need? Where
might that help and
support come from?

Write an alternative gift list, noting all the things you will
need, not to set up your home or upgrade your stuff (!), but
to sustain your marriage for a lifetime. Would you like
more patience? Health? Fulfilment? Less busyness?

Choosing your readings

At this point in the service, you will be able to sit down and hear one or more readings, one of which needs to be from the Bible. You can really personalize this part of your wedding, so it's worth spending some time together thinking about what you would like to hear on your special day.

It can be hard to know where to start with passages from the Bible, so on the next few pages you will find three of the most popular, in a modern translation, together with some ideas to get you thinking about what they mean. There are many more to choose from, of course - **http://yourchurchwedding.org** is a great place to find not only Bible extracts but poetry, too.

When you're choosing a reading, think about the following:
- What themes do you think are most important? These are personal to you, but might include togetherness, love, commitment, forgiveness, family and children.
- Who will be doing the reading - a friend, a relative or perhaps even you? Try your potential passages aloud to each other.
- Are your readings really just for you, or do they express what you want to say to your family and friends? There may be some that you want to keep for yourself, and others that you want to share.

Remember to discuss all your readings with your minister.

The Bible at your wedding: 1 Corinthians 13

If I speak in the tongues of mortals and of angels, but do not have love, I am a noisy gong or a clanging cymbal. And if I have prophetic powers, and understand all mysteries and all knowledge, and if I have all faith, so as to remove mountains, but do not have love, I am nothing. . . . Love is patient; love is kind; love is not envious or boastful or arrogant or rude. It does not insist on its own way; it is not irritable or resentful; it does not rejoice in wrongdoing, but rejoices in the truth. It bears all things, believes all things, hopes all things, endures all things. Love never ends. . . . And now faith, hope, and love abide, these three; and the greatest of these is love.

Slowly breathe in, and then out. Imagine you are breathing in God's gift of love, and breathing it out into the world around you. Inspiration literally means 'breathing in'. In this reading, love is the inspiration of all the good things we do, think and say. The air we breathe goes first to our muscles and brain and then out of our mouth so that we can move, think and speak. In the same way, we can 'breathe in' God's love, and then let that love guide our actions, thoughts and words.

Try substituting your own names for the word 'love' in this reading. What do you learn about yourself and each other? Now read it again, using just your fiancé(e)'s name.

'_____ is **patient**; _____ is **kind**; she/he is **not envious** or **boastful** or **arrogant** or **rude**.'

The Bible at your wedding:
John 2.1-10

On the third day there was a wedding in Cana of Galilee, and the mother of Jesus was there. Jesus and his disciples had also been invited to the wedding. When the wine gave out, the mother of Jesus said to him, 'They have no wine.' And Jesus said to her, 'Woman, what concern is that to you and to me? My hour has not yet come.' His mother said to the servants, 'Do whatever he tells you.' Now standing there were six stone water-jars for the Jewish rites of purification, each holding twenty or thirty gallons. Jesus said to them, 'Fill the jars with water.' And they filled them up to the brim. . . . When the steward tasted the water that had become wine, . . . the steward called the bridegroom and said to him, 'Everyone serves the good wine first, and then the inferior wine after the guests have become drunk. But you have kept the good wine until now.'

This couple must have been glad that they had invited Jesus! All relationships go through times when they feel as if they've run dry, when the joy just isn't there. Have you experienced such moments already?

Have a glass of wine or some other favourite drink together. Tell each other what makes you feel most alive, joyful, blessed - as individuals and as a couple. Resolve never to lose sight of those things.

The Bible at your wedding: Colossians 3.12-15

As God's chosen ones, holy and beloved, clothe yourselves with compassion, kindness, humility, meekness, and patience. Bear with one another and, if anyone has a complaint against another, forgive each other; just as the Lord has forgiven you, so you also must forgive. Above all, clothe yourselves with love, which binds everything together in perfect harmony. And let the peace of Christ rule in your hearts, to which indeed you were called in the one body. And be thankful.

At your wedding, everyone will probably be in their best clothes, as a way of celebrating with you and honouring you on your special day. Think about how you went about choosing your own clothes for the occasion.

This reading imagines that we can put on kindness, gentleness, patience and love as if they were beautiful clothes. As you get dressed on an ordinary day, try thinking about how you are preparing mentally, emotionally and spiritually for the challenges you will face. What virtues will you need in order to live well - patience, integrity, tolerance, courage? How might you 'clothe yourselves' in those virtues right at the start of each day? Which of your emotional and spiritual items of clothing are the easiest to put on? And which are the hardest?

The Vows: actions speak louder than words

Sometimes, the father of the bride is invited to come forward and place the bride's hand in the groom's hand. This isn't 'giving the bride away', but is an act of trust that the couple will care for each other as a new family. If you feel that this tradition isn't for you, there are other options, so do talk to your minister about them.

..... and ......, I now invite you to join hands and make your vows, in the presence of God and his people. *The bride and bridegroom face each other. The bridegroom takes the bride's right hand in his.*

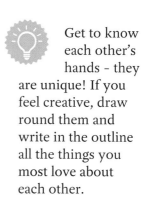

Joining hands in marriage isn't like the handshake that seals a business contract, when two people close a deal. Instead, it is a free act of giving and receiving.

Think about the hands that have held you and that you have held during your life: those of parents, grandparents, brothers, sisters and friends. How have these people helped you to become the person you are? Have you ever been let down by those who were supposed to care for you? How has that affected your ability to trust others? How have you dealt with this in your relationship?

Get to know each other's hands - they are unique! If you feel creative, draw round them and write in the outline all the things you most love about each other.

The Vows: words are important too

These are the most famous words in the marriage service. Through the centuries, couples have pledged their love and commitment to each other in these very words.

I, ... , take you, ... ,
to be my wife (husband),
to have and to hold
from this day forward;
for better, for worse,
for richer, for poorer,
in sickness and in health,
to love and to cherish,
till death us do part;
according to God's holy law.
In the presence of God
I make this vow.

For better, for worse . . .

When two people make a commitment to each other, it can involve sacrifices. You might make them willingly, but it can be good to name and honour them, without turning it into an opportunity to score points!

How has your relationship changed your life? What changes have been for the better? Are you aware of having given anything up? What sacrifices or compromises do you each make so that your quality of life as a couple is as good as it can possibly be?

We both turned down promotion because relocating to be closer to each other was more important.

Separately, write down the five most important things about your life together, and then share your lists with each other.

. . . for richer, for poorer . . .

Sadly, some relationships do break down, and often it's disagreements about money that are to blame. Taking time before your wedding to think together about what money means to you, and how you will manage your money as a couple, is time well spent.

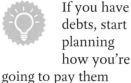

How have your attitudes towards money been shaped by your past, especially by your upbringing? Share some of your assumptions with each other.

- Are you spenders or savers?
- How do you feel about buying things on credit?
- Will you have a joint account, separate accounts or both?
- Does either of you have any debts at the moment, or a history of getting into debt?
- If you have any spare cash at the end of the month, what do you do with it?
- How do you each feel about giving to charity? Is your charitable giving organized (e.g. through standing orders)?
- If you already live together, how did setting up home change your finances or your attitudes to money?

If you have debts, start planning how you're going to pay them off. Consider seeing a financial adviser. If you haven't already made a will, you should *definitely* make one.

. . . in sickness and in health . . .

If you or someone close to you has major health problems, these words may be particularly significant to you. Couples who have been through illness together often speak of the way it has drawn them closer and helped them appreciate life.

You may have been fortunate enough to have little or no first-hand experience of serious illness. But even minor illnesses teach us a lot about ourselves and how we react to suffering, adversity and the challenges that life brings. With the passing years, our bodies change - even if we keep our health, we might lose fitness,

We postponed our wedding when I found out I had a heart defect. It was scary, but we grew stronger together through it.

change shape and get wrinkles. While we should enjoy the vitality we have, we can also appreciate that real love is more than skin deep.

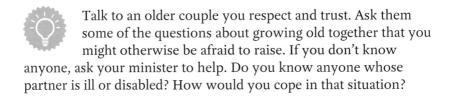

Share with each other any first-hand experiences you have of significant illness, whether physical or mental. How did you cope? What helped? What was hardest to deal with? It is worth sharing such problems, even though it might be difficult to do so. This is especially true of mental illness due to the stigma it carries.

Talk to an older couple you respect and trust. Ask them some of the questions about growing old together that you might otherwise be afraid to raise. If you don't know anyone, ask your minister to help. Do you know anyone whose partner is ill or disabled? How would you cope in that situation?

. . . to love and to cherish, till death us do part . . .

'Cherish' feels like a special word: we don't often use it in everyday conversation, so it's worth thinking about what it means to you. Cherishing someone might not be about the grand gestures, big decisions and great sacrifices; instead, it is often seen in the small, ordinary things. It's these that smooth the edges of your relationship and help you feel just as loving in your married life as you did on your wedding day. The way 'cherishing' looks in your life is personal to you as a couple.

How do you cherish each other now? How did you cherish each other when you first fell in love? How might you cherish each other in five years' time, or in your old age?

Separately, write a list of little things you can do for each other that will make the other person feel special, loved and cherished, and resolve to do one of them each day. Revise the list regularly!

My husband was always so patient and gentle putting in my eye drops every morning and evening. It made the treatment bearable.

We seem to be so busy, but we make sure we're both in on a Friday night. When the kids have gone to bed, we open a bottle of wine, snuggle on the sofa and watch a DVD - bliss!

... in the presence of God I make this vow

Getting married in church means you are making your vows in the house of God and in the presence of God. Couples choose a church wedding for all sorts of reasons, some hard to put into words. But it can be good to talk together before your wedding about why a church wedding feels important to you.

Everyone's experience of God and church is unique. Here are some of the feelings that other couples have expressed about marrying in church. Do any of them strike a chord with you? Is there anything you'd like to add?

A wedding seems to mean more and feel more special if it takes place in church.

My parents married in this church, too, so we feel we're part of something bigger; our wedding isn't just about us.

A church wedding is the right way to get married - I don't think I'd feel properly married if it wasn't in church.

We always knew we wanted a church wedding, and it's been good to meet the Sunday congregation and to know they are supporting us and thinking of us at this special time.

The Giving of Rings

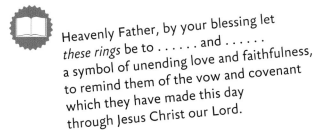

Heavenly Father, by your blessing let *these rings* be to . . . . . . and . . . . . . a symbol of unending love and faithfulness, to remind them of the vow and covenant which they have made this day through Jesus Christ our Lord.
Amen.

Hold the ring on your fiancé(e)'s finger as you say the following words. This helps the action, the ring, the words, your emotions and God's blessing come together to make this moment something that will stay with you your whole life.

. . . . . . , I give you this ring as a sign of our marriage. With my body I honour you, all that I am I give to you, and all that I have I share with you.

If you will both be having a wedding ring, take it in turns to hold your own and each other's ring in your hand. Feel the metal turn warm and trace the circle with your finger. In your mind and heart, fill the ring or rings with your love for each other.

Because a ring is round, with no corners and no end, it is said to go on for ever, a symbol of everlasting love. Gold or other precious metals show that the ring represents something incorruptible and infinitely precious – a whole person, given in love to another.

All that I am I give to you . . .

Most of us hide aspects of ourselves in daily life - this is normal and helps protect us from getting hurt. But marriage is a relationship in which you trust each other with the person you really are inside. Some people find it harder than others to share their real selves. If you have trusted someone before and been hurt, then it can be hard to let someone into your life again. It may even be that your fiancé(e) will be the first person who has ever really and truly known you.

Just be yourself? If only . . .

In marriage, there is no holding back - the person your fiancé(e) has fallen in love with is the real you. This is a great gift!

Talk as a couple about the situations in which you feel you have to pretend, put on a mask or conform to expectations. You may find it helpful to complete these sentences:

- At work, I have to be. . . .

- For my parents, I have to be . . .

- My friends expect me to be . . .

- I sometimes feel I ought to be . . .

- But with you, I can be . . .

. . . and all that I have I share with you

Remember the words of St Paul (page 14): love doesn't insist on its own way. 'All that you have' doesn't just mean the stuff you've accumulated so far and the money you earn. It's also your time, your energy, your talents . . . When you belong to each other in marriage, your time, talents and energy are shared resources, and deciding how they are 'spent' may often need to be a joint decision.

Spend some time naming each other's best qualities – the person's particular gifts, skills and personality traits. Enjoy the characteristics you have in common, and think about those areas where you complement or make up for each other.

Look again at one of the best-loved Bible readings for weddings, 1 Corinthians 13 (see page 14). Start with the characteristics of love that are listed in this reading. How many of them apply to either of you? Then think about other words you would want to add to make the reading a good description of each of you.

People always think that we get on well because we're really similar, but it's amazing how our differences have made our lives so much richer than they were before.

Celebrating each other's gifts is really important. Otherwise, when you get used to someone, you can end up just taking them for granted.

The Proclamation

In the presence of God, and before this congregation,
...... and ...... have given their consent
and made their marriage vows to each other.
They have declared their marriage by the joining of hands
and by the giving and receiving of *rings*.
I therefore proclaim that they are husband and wife.

The release of tension at this point in the service is often expressed in a spontaneous round of applause, and you may be invited to exchange a kiss. Enjoy this moment!

The minister joins their right hands together and says
Those whom God has joined together let no one put asunder.

The minister may use a stole (a decorated scarf) to join your hands. The stole is a symbol of the Church's enduring support for your marriage, enabling it to last a lifetime. This is your desire, the Church's desire, and God's desire, and you will probably want to focus on building a lasting marriage rather than planning for failure. This will involve:

Good communication: many of the talking tasks in this book are also listening tasks! Expressing your feelings and paying attention to each other's feelings is crucial.

Friendship: lasts beyond the initial chemistry - but your sexual union with each other is also an important way of deepening your relationship.

Forgiveness: this means being willing to let go of grudges and to draw a line under arguments - don't let them fester.

Honesty: accept each other for who you really are.

The Blessing of the Marriage

There are several different blessings that your minister may use. This is an important moment in your wedding service, so ask your minister to show you the options and think about which you like best.

Count your blessings!
If you believe that God has given you to each other, then say 'thank you' – he's given you someone amazing! As you reflect on your life together so far, think of all the ways in which you have been blessed. These might include:

- somewhere to live
- family and friends to support you
- work that you enjoy
- interests and hobbies, especially those you share
- children, if you've already started a family of your own.

What about the difficult stuff?
If your situation is complicated or difficult, your blessings may be harder to spot, or they may stand out more clearly. It can be helpful to talk to your minister:

- if you have been recently bereaved;
- if you want to have children, but you know you can't;
- if you struggle with physical or mental health issues;
- if there are people close to you who don't support your marriage.

The Registration of the Marriage

Church marriage registers are kept 'in perpetuity', which means for ever! Church archives contain ancient registers dating back many centuries. Your marriage and the details of your families become a part of that living history.

Marriage is a change of status in the eyes of the law. People will see you differently and usually have to get used to the bride's new name! There can be implications for tax, inheritance or even nationality.

What a difference a day makes . . . What do you think will feel different once you are married? For example, if you have been living together for a long time, what difference will your new married status make? If you already have children, are you planning to change their surnames?

Look at the 'Your Marriage' section of the website **http://yourchurchwedding.org** for more information on all these matters, and think through whether there are any practical things you need to do.

Prayers

What are your deepest concerns as you approach your wedding?
And as you think about your life together?

If you are not used to praying regularly, it can seem daunting to
write your own prayer. But praying doesn't have to be complicated
or use special words. It is really just talking to God about things that
are on your mind. You might find this page helpful as you think
about what you would like to include in the prayers. Reflect
separately and then talk together about this, then share your ideas
with your minister - he or she may be able to use some of them in
the service.

When we think of our situation now, we are thankful for . . .

In our life now, we are concerned about . . .

When we think about the future, we look forward to . . .

When we think about the future, we worry about . . .

**When we think of the people around us, our friends and
families, we hope for . . .**

When we look around at the world, we worry about . . .

And we are thankful for . . .

**When we have been married for a long time, we hope that
we will be . . .**

The Lord's Prayer

The prayers conclude with the Lord's Prayer.

This is the prayer that Jesus taught his friends when they asked him to teach them to pray. It's both a prayer in itself and a useful pattern for prayer. The words are well known, and often it is words like these that remind us that we are all part of something bigger than we are. There is also a version of the prayer in more modern English – ask your minister to show you both so you can decide which you would like to use in your wedding service.

Our Father, who art in heaven,
hallowed be thy name;
thy kingdom come;
thy will be done;
on earth as it is in heaven.
Give us this day our daily bread.
And forgive us our trespasses,
as we forgive those who
trespass against us.
And lead us not into temptation;
but deliver us from evil.
For thine is the kingdom,
the power and the glory,
for ever and ever.
Amen.

Words that stand the test of time . . .

Share with each other any prayers or quotations that bring you comfort or inspire you. These may be words you remember from childhood, or that have become special to you recently.

The first day of the rest of your life . . .

The marriage service ends with a blessing for you and for all those who have come to support you. It's a reminder that your minister and church will carry on praying for you long after your wedding, and that God's blessing on you also lasts a lifetime.

Your church would love to keep in touch with you - don't forget to tell your minister if you move house, or if you have exciting news to share, or if you need some help.

If you move to a new area, remember that churches can be great places to find out what's going on locally, and a good source of support as you start your married life. A minister would be delighted to come and bless your new home, too! You can find your local churches here; **www.achurchnearyou.com**

Above all, celebrate your marriage - make the most of your anniversaries; and why not think about renewing your vows after 5 years, or after 10, 25 or 50 years?

Where to find help when you need it

All relationships, and all families, go through challenging times as well as good times. That's why the vows talk about marriage being 'for better, for worse'. Realizing when you need to ask for some extra help shows that you value your marriage and your life together – and there is no shame in that!

Your local church promises to be there for you. This means it will not only celebrate with you when things are going well, but also walk alongside you in the tough times. Your local minister – even if he or she isn't the person who married you – can often help you work out where to get the assistance you need.

We're interested in exploring the Christian faith . . . Ask your minister or take a look at the church's website to see if there are any groups or courses available. Also see: **www.rejesus.co.uk**

We just need a bit of support . . . The Mothers' Union (**www.themothersunion.org**) offers parenting courses, family respite, family holidays and much more.

We're worried about money . . . Various organizations offer advice on budgeting, and can aid you as you sort out your finances: Christians Against Poverty (**https://capuk.org**) is a national debt counselling charity with a network of 190 centres based in local churches.

It's all going wrong . . . If your relationship gets into difficulties, it's often better to get help sooner rather than later. Relate (**www.relate.org.uk**) offers advice, workshops, relationship counselling, sex therapy, consultations, mediation and support.

First published in Great Britain in 2014

Society for Promoting Christian Knowledge
36 Causton Street
London SW1P 4ST
www.spckpublishing.co.uk

British Library Cataloguing-in-Publication Data
A catalogue record for this book is available from the British Library

ISBN 978-0-281-07071-8
eBook ISBN 978-0-281-07135-7

1 3 5 7 9 10 8 6 4 2

Designed by Sarah Smith
Typeset by Graphicraft Limited, Hong Kong
Printed in Great Britain by Micropress Printers Ltd

eBook by Graphicraft Limited, Hong Kong

Produced on paper from sustainable forests

So you're planning a church wedding. The date and reception venue are fixed and the other details are falling into place. Now it's time to focus on the service itself, and preparing for your married life beyond the big day.

The aim of this booklet is to enable you to *make the most* of your wedding day. It uses the words and actions of the marriage service, as well as questions and activities to help you think about life, family, God, relationships, commitment, church and more.

The Revd Ally Barrett is Vicar of Buckden and Offord, Cambridgeshire, and loves helping couples to prepare for their wedding day. She is a mum to two young children and is a fan of sci-fi and Marmite. She is also the author of *Making the Most of Your Child's Baptism*.

ISBN 978-0-281-07071-8

9 780281 070718

www.spckpublishing.co.uk

Cover design by Sarah Smith

Cover images: © HayleyRuth Photography, Sean Og, Sophie Stanes and Shutterstock.